First Lessons in Math

written by Eunice M. Magos
and Esther H. Hornnes
illustrated by Priscilla Burris

EUNICE M. MAGOS received a Bachelor of Science degree from New York University, and a Master's degree in Individualized Education from the College of St. Scholastica in Minnesota. She has been a director of Head Start, taught gifted primary classes and participated in the Learning to Read Through the Arts program. She has taught remedial reading and kindergarten and currently teaches first grade in the Hopatcong Borough School District in New Jersey.

ESTHER H. HORNNES received a Bachelor of Arts degree from Shelton College and William Paterson College in New Jersey. She has done graduate work at North Dakota State University and Oslo University in Oslo, Norway. She has taught grades 1-4 and presently teaches pre-school in the Hillside Nursery School in Succasunna, New Jersey.

PRISCILLA BURRIS received an Associate of Arts Degree in Creative Design from the Fashion Institute of Design and Merchandising in Los Angeles. As a free lance artist of child-related artwork, she has been drawing since she was one year old. Priscilla lives in southern California.

Reproduction of these pages by the classroom teacher for use in the classroom and not for commercial use is permissible. Reproduction of these pages for an entire school or school district is strictly prohibited.

Copyright 1987 by **THE MONKEY SISTERS, INC.**
22971 Via Cruz
Laguna Niguel, CA 92677

ISBN 0-933606-49-4

FIRST LESSONS IN MATH

These beginning lessons contain large numbers and graphics to easily introduce young learners to numbers, sets, shapes and counting.

Each number 1-10 includes a take-home manipulative project as well as practice in tracing and writing the number.

CONTENTS   Page

Counting 1	1
Recognizing number 1	2
Counting 2	3
Recognizing sets of 2	4
Matching numbers to sets 1-2	5
Counting 3	6
Recognizing sets of 3	7
Counting 4	8
Recognizing number 4	9
Review: Counting sets 1-4	10
Counting 5	11
Recognizing sets of 5	12
Counting 6	13
Recognizing sets of 6	14
Numerical order 1-6	15
Counting 7	16
Recognizing sets of 7	17
Counting 8	18
Recognizing sets of 8	19
Counting 9	20
Recognizing sets of 9	21
Counting 10	22
Recognizing sets of 10	23
Numerical order 1-10	24
Recognizing shapes; following directions	25
Reviewing shapes	26
Reviewing shapes; following directions	27
Digital time on the hour	28
Digital time on the hour	29
Measuring for recipes	30
Measuring ½ of an object	31
Picture story problems-addition	32
Picture story problems-subtraction	33
Graphing	34
Matching sets to numbers 1-10	35
Writing number words 1-5	36
Writing number words 6-10	37

Skill: Counting 1   Name _____

Directions: Children count one sun. Class may learn short poem on visor. Children color and cut out visor and attach strips for head band to use as a take-home activity.

First Lessons in Math © THE MONKEY SISTERS, INC.

Skill: Recognizing number 1

Name _____

Directions: Children count 1 dragon, trace 1, write 1's on line and color dragon.

First Lessons in Math © THE MONKEY SISTERS, INC.

Skill: Counting 2

Name _____

2

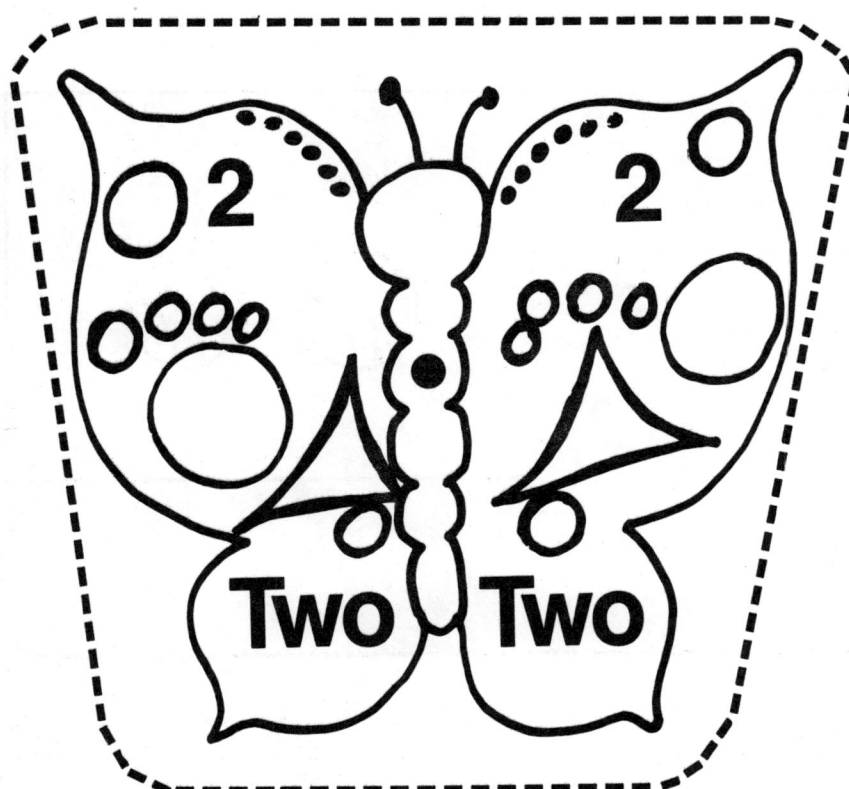

Directions: Children color and cut out the two butterflies on the dotted lines. Attach each butterfly to a 12-inch string through black dot in center. Children can have fun flying their butterflies outside.

First Lessons in Math © THE MONKEY SISTERS, INC.

Skill: Recognizing sets of 2

Name _____

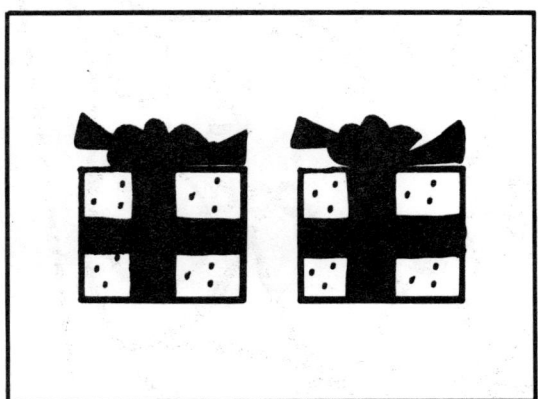 

2

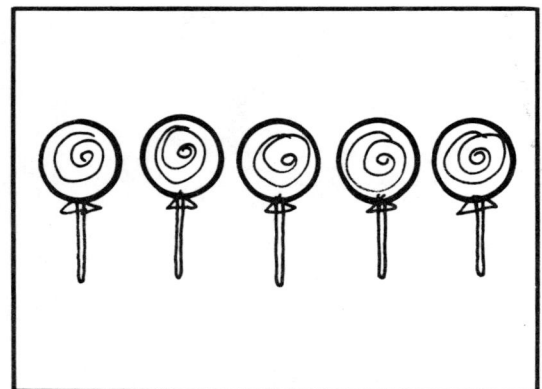 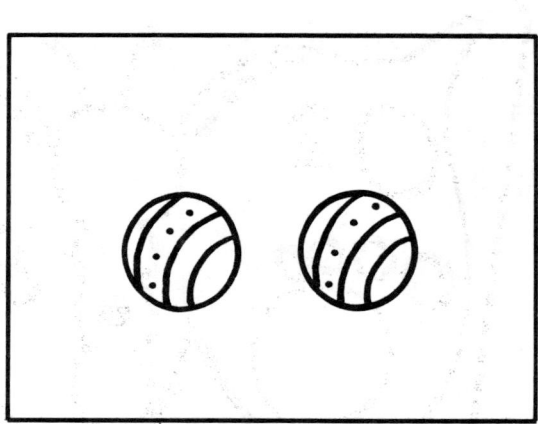

2 2 _____

Directions: Children count and color the sets that show 2, trace 2 and write 2's on the line.

First Lessons in Math © THE MONKEY SISTERS, INC.

Skill: Matching numbers to sets 1-2

Name _____

1
2
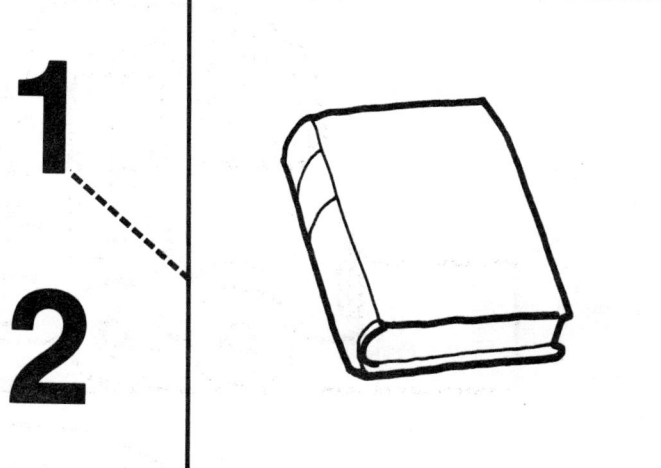

1
2

1
2

Directions: Children draw a line from the number to the correct set. Color sets of 1 red. Color sets of 2 blue.

First Lessons in Math © THE MONKEY SISTERS, INC.

Skill: Counting 3

Name _____

3   Three

Directions: Children count three vehicles and color them. Cut out on solid black lines and fold back on dotted lines to make stand-ups.

First Lessons in Math © THE MONKEY SISTERS, INC.

Skill: Recognizing sets of 3

Name _____

3	
3	 
3	  

Directions: Children count sets of 3, trace 3, write 3's on line and color sets of 3.

First Lessons in Math © THE MONKEY SISTERS, INC.

Skill: Counting 4

Name _____

4   Four

Directions: Children count the set of four. Color and cut out the four finger puppets. Practice telling the story of "Goldilocks and the Three Bears."

First Lessons in Math © THE MONKEY SISTERS, INC.

Skill: Recognizing number 4

Name _____

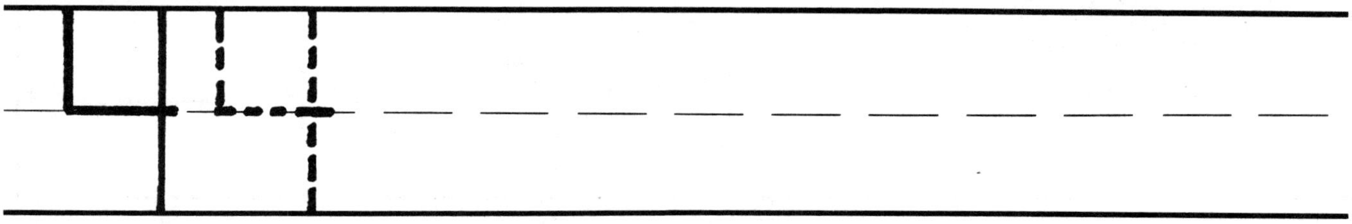

Directions: Children count kittens and bowls of milk. Draw a line to match a kitten to each bowl of milk. Trace number 4, write 4's on line.

Skill: Counting sets 1-4

Name _____

Count and write: 1, 2, 3 or 4

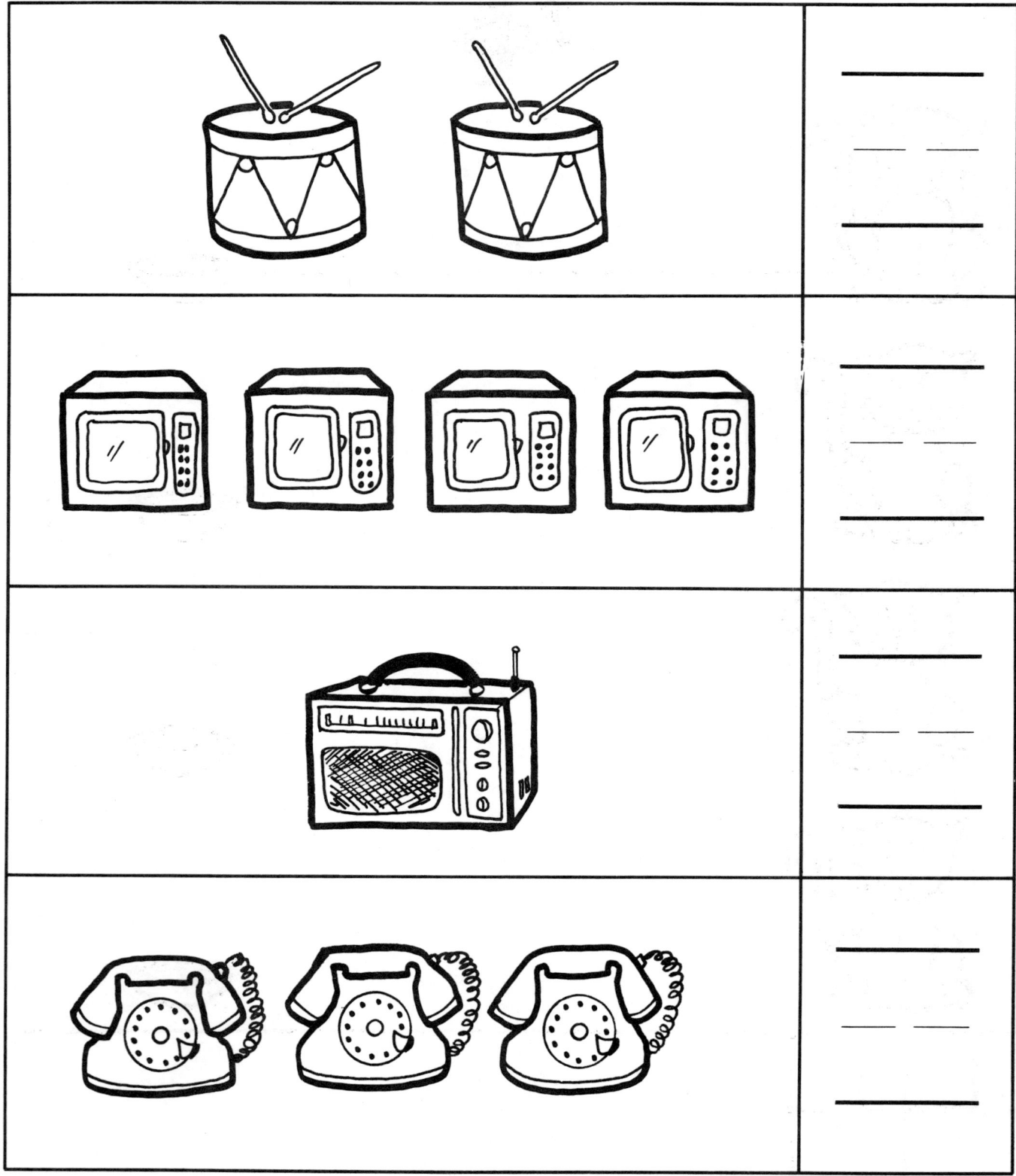

Directions: Children write the number that tells how many objects are in each set.

Skill: Counting 5   Name _____

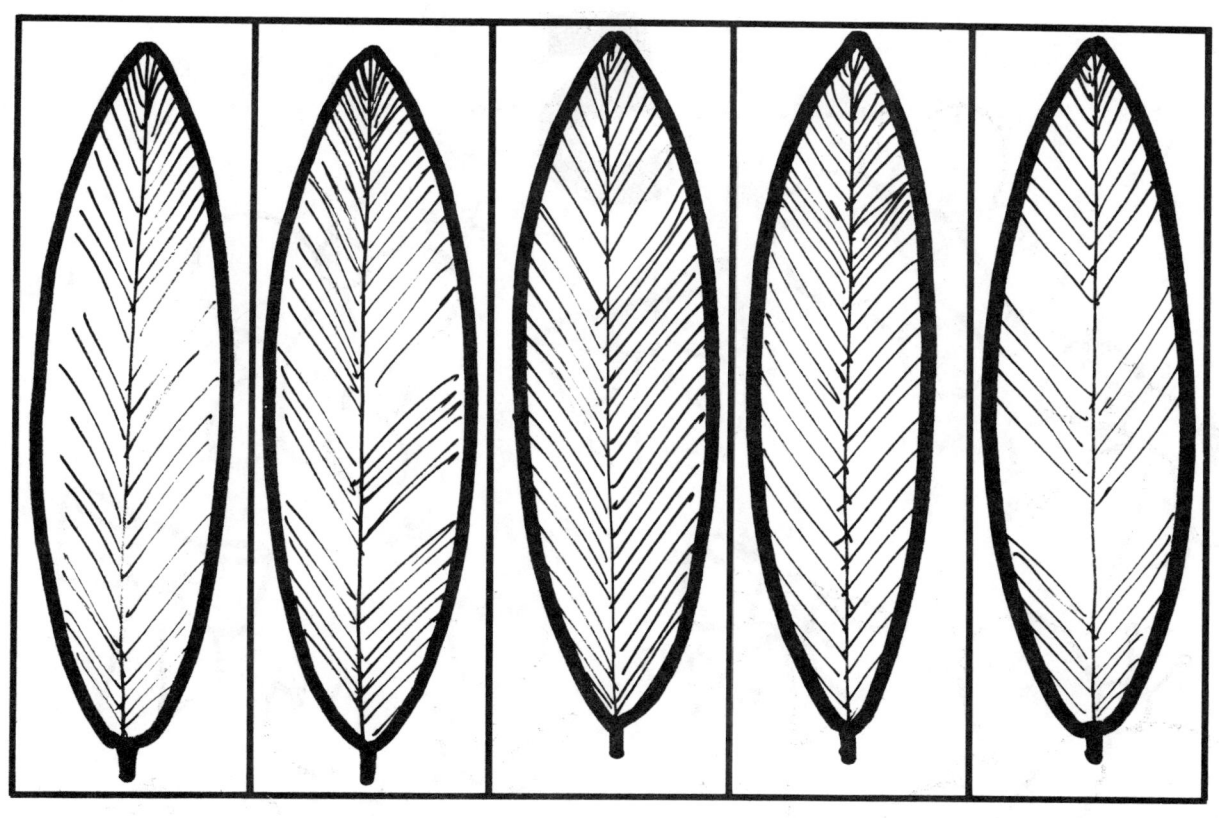

Directions: Children count feathers. Color sets of 5 on headband. Color feathers.
Cut out feathers and headband on heavy lines. Paste headband together. Attach feathers.

First Lessons in Math © THE MONKEY SISTERS, INC.

Skill: Recognizing sets of 5

Name _____

Directions: Children color 5 butterflies orange. Color 5 tulips red. Color 5 bows blue. Trace number 5, write 5's on line.

First Lessons in Math © THE MONKEY SISTERS, INC.

Skill: Counting 6

Name _____

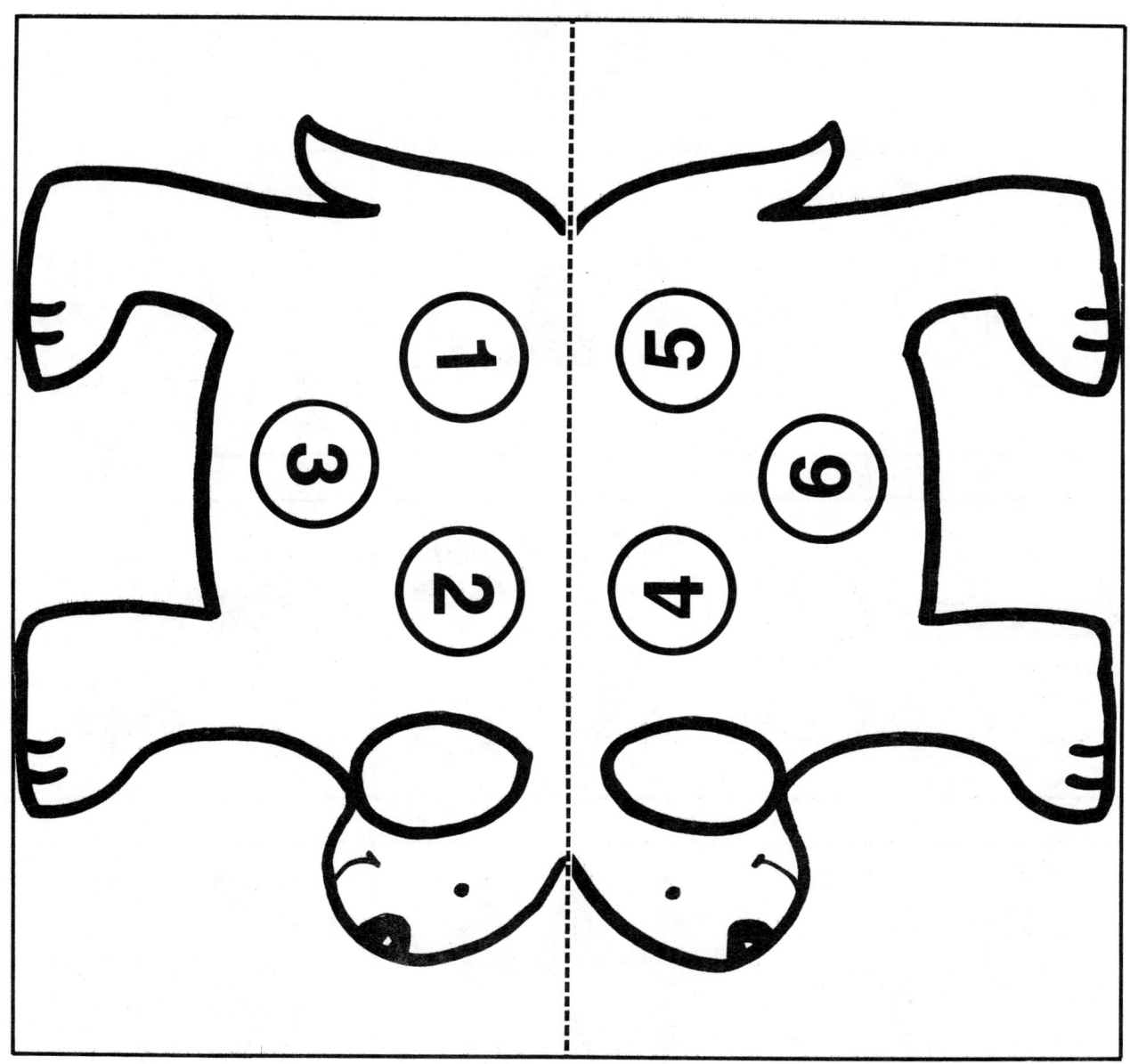

6 Six

Directions: Children color the six spots on Rover. Cut around the outline of the dog or cut on the heavy line which forms a rectangle. Fold on dotted line to make dog stand.

Skill: Recognizing sets of 6   Name _____

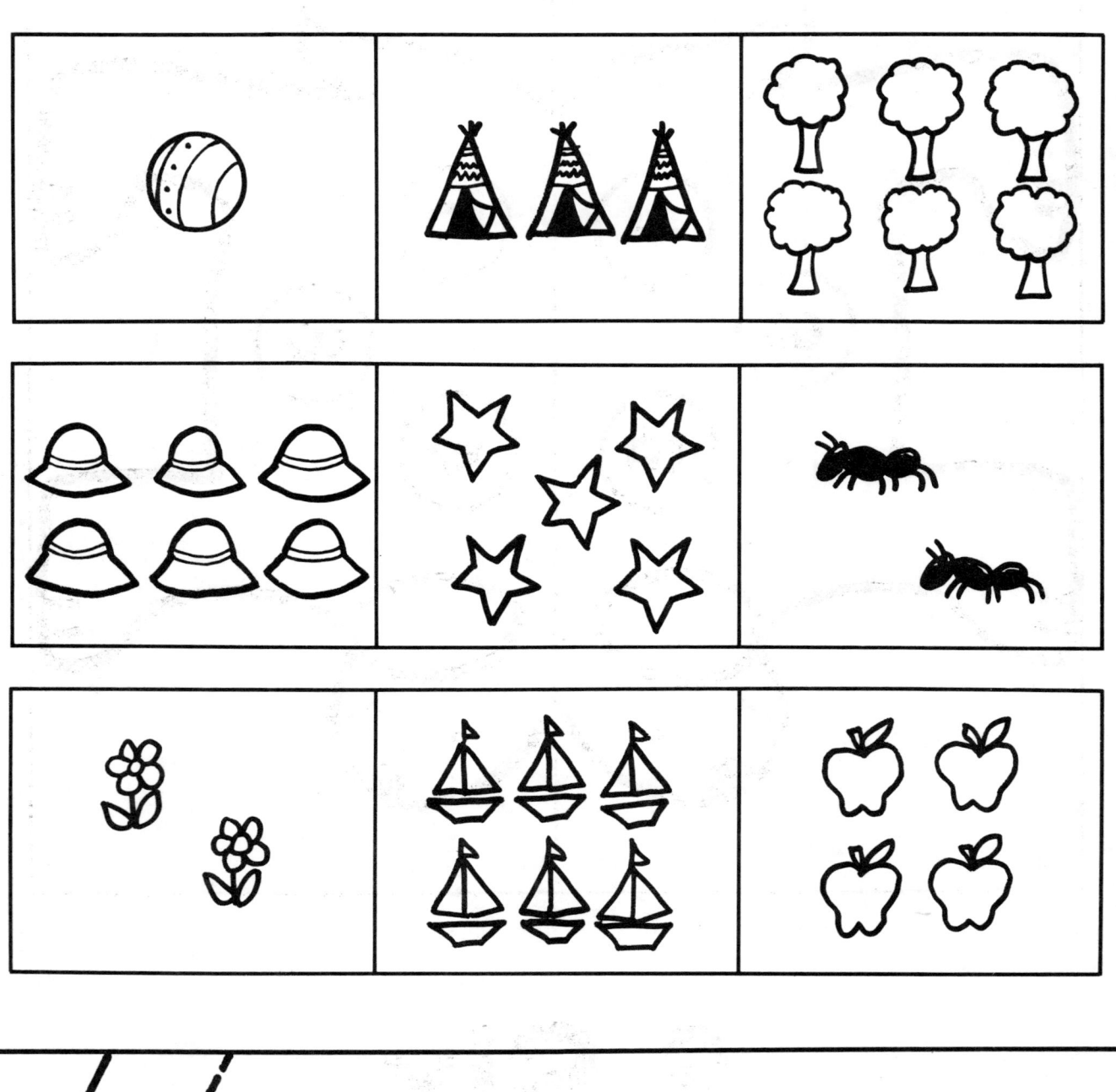

Directions: Children color the boxes that show sets of six. Trace 6, write 6's on line.

Skill: Numerical order 1-6

Name _____

Directions: Children cut out numbers below. Glue in the correct squares above.

First Lessons in Math © THE MONKEY SISTERS, INC.

15.

Skill: Counting 7

Name _____

7 Seven

Directions: Children color the seal and the balls. Cut out circle on heavy line and attach in back of seal at *X*'s with fastener. Children count the balls as the seal balances them.

First Lessons in Math © THE MONKEY SISTERS, INC.

Skill: Recognizing sets of 7

Name _____

Directions: Happy Clown is missing his balloons. Children find the ballons with 7 dots. Cut out on the heavy lines. Paste over dotted balloons. Trace 7, write 7's on line.

Skill: Counting 8

Name _____

Count my legs!

8 Eight

Directions: Children color the spider's body and legs (strips) black. Cut the four strips apart and cutout the spider's body. Criss-cross the strips. Place the body on top of the strips and staple in the center on the black dot. You can attach an elastic thread or rubber band as you staple and it will bounce up and down.

First Lessons in Math © THE MONKEY SISTERS, INC.

Skill: Recognizing sets of 8

Name _____

8

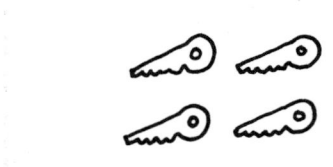

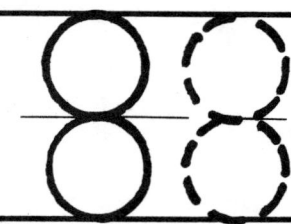

Directions: Children count the number of items in each box and write the number on the line. Children then draw a continuous line from the first box of ice cream cones to each box that contain sets of eight. Trace 8, write 8's on line.

First Lessons in Math © THE MONKEY SISTERS, INC.

Skill: Counting 9   Name _____

9 Nine

Directions: Children count and color the happy faces. Cut out fan on heavy lines. Fan-fold on dotted lines. Staple at bottom.

First Lessons in Math © THE MONKEY SISTERS, INC.

Skill: Recognizing sets of 9   Name _____

Color 9

Color 9

Directions: Children color 9 in each row. Trace 9, write 9's on line.

First Lessons in Math © THE MONKEY SISTERS, INC.

Skill: Counting 10

Name _____

10 Ten

Directions: Children color each numbered section and count as they color. Cut on the outside curved lines. Punch a hole at the • and string yarn through to make a neckpiece to wear.

Skill: Recognizing sets of 10

Name _____

10

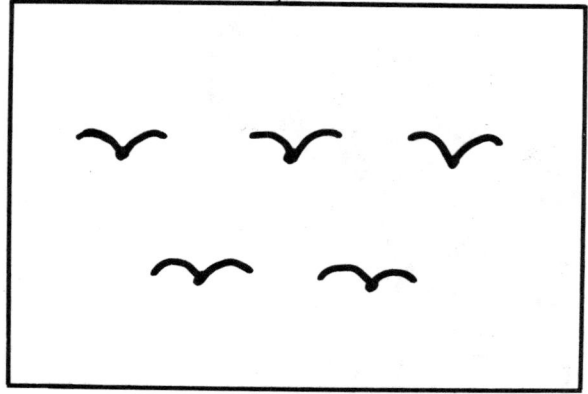

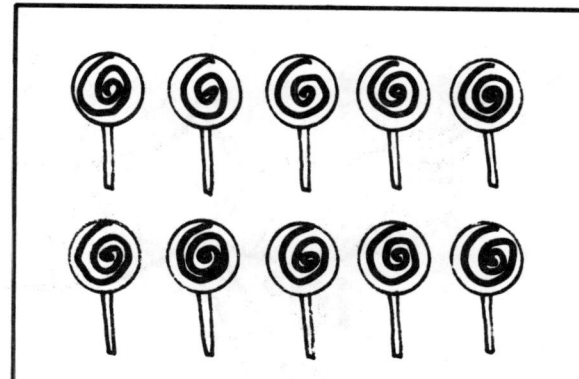

_____   _____

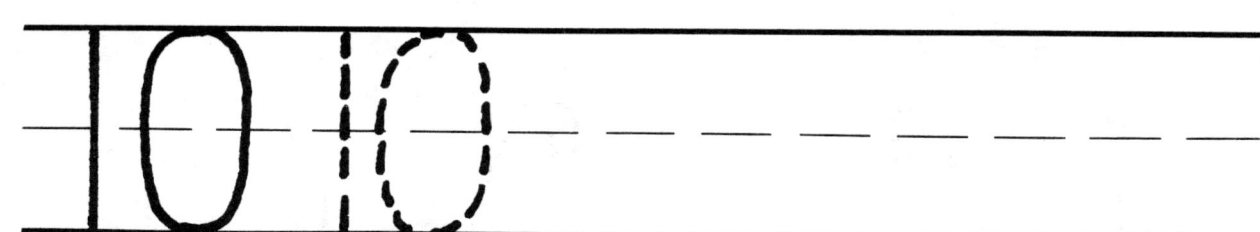

_____

Directions: Children write the number 10 on the line under the illustration which shows 10 items. Trace 10, write 10's on line.

First Lessons in Math © THE MONKEY SISTERS, INC.

Skill: Numerical order 1-10

Name _____

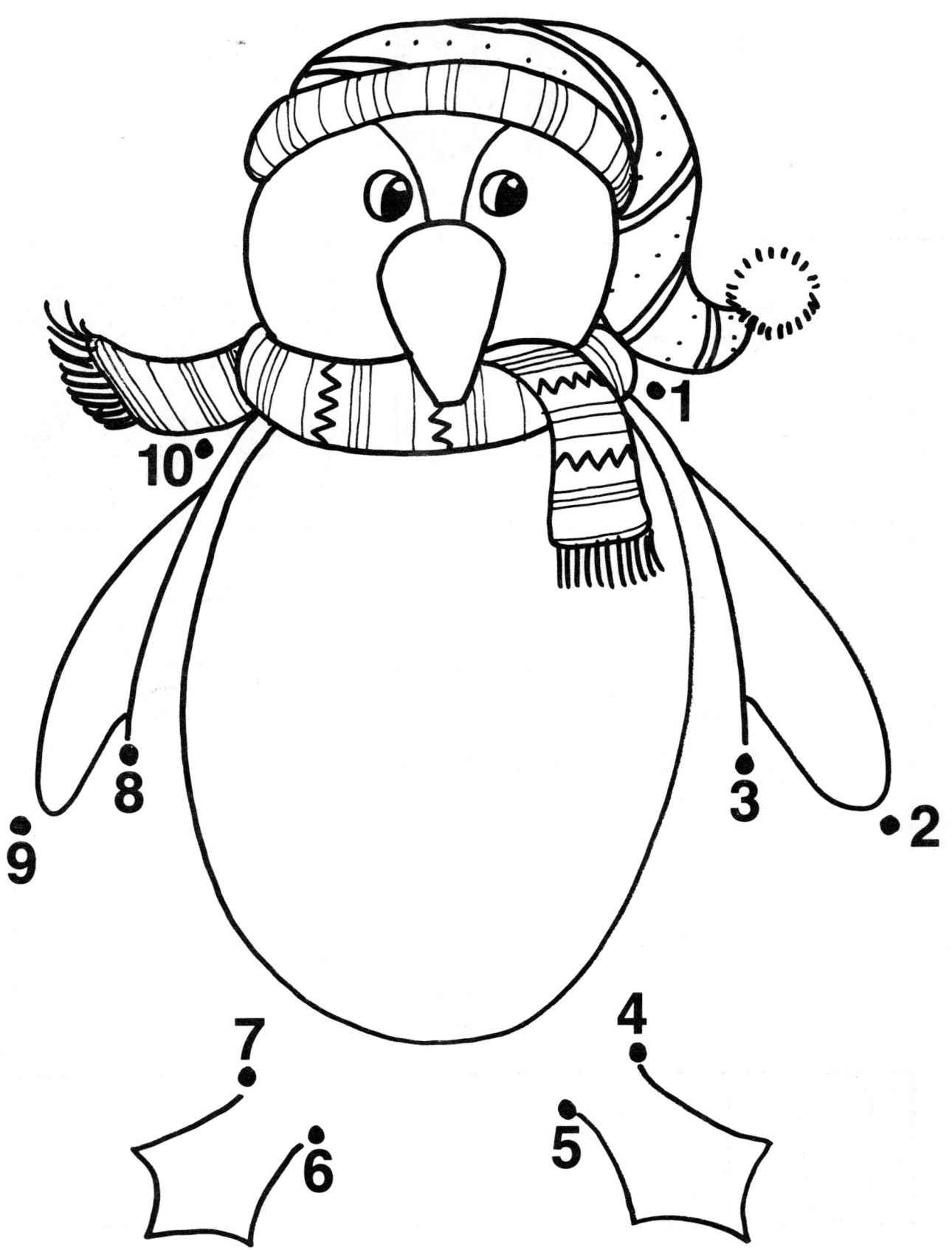

Directions: Children connect the dots in order from 1 to 10. Color the picture.

Skill: Recognizing shapes; following directions

Name _____

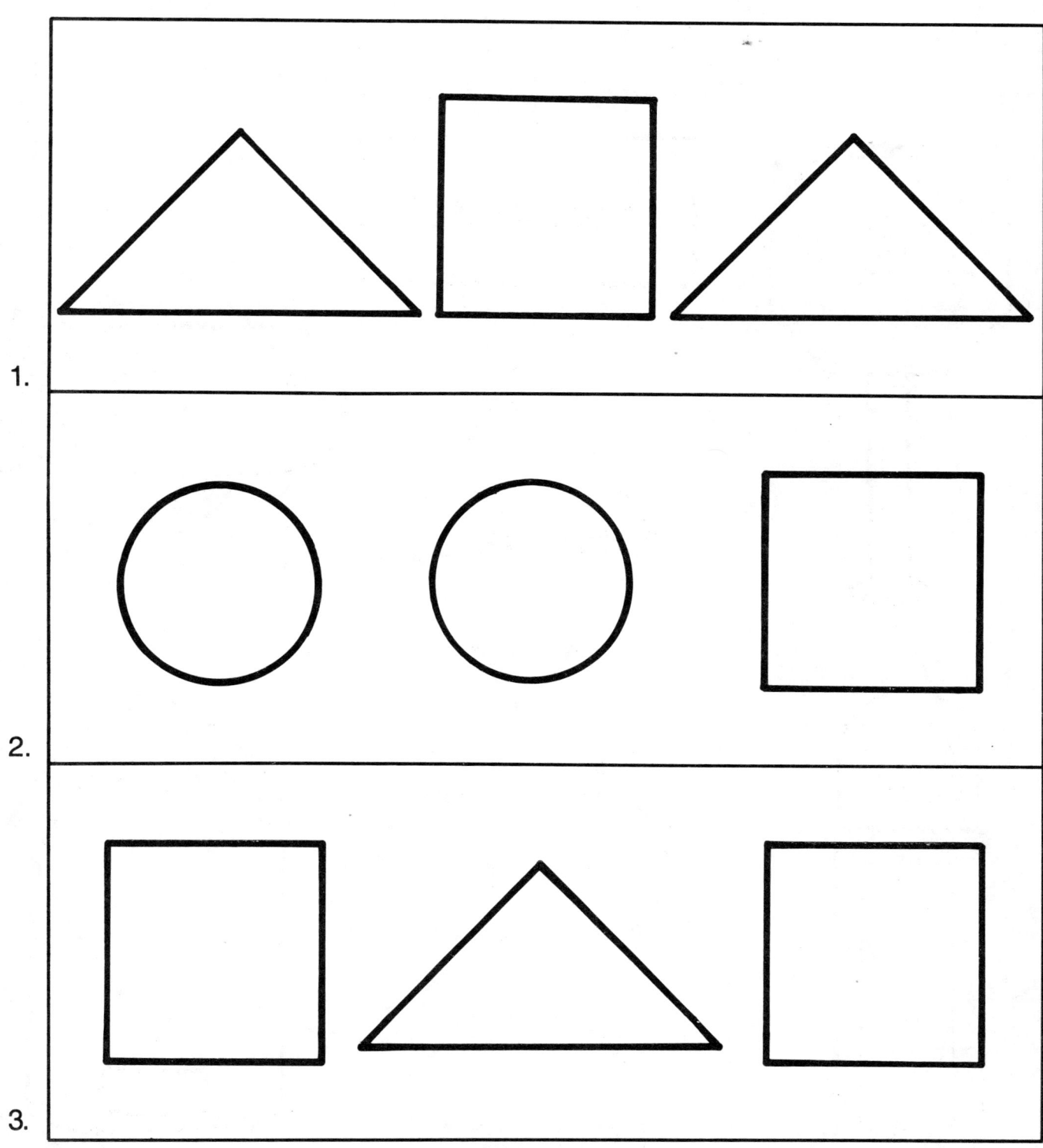

1.
2.
3.

Directions: Read orally to children: Row 1: Put a blue X on the triangles.
Row 2: Draw a red line under the circles.
Row 3: Color the squares green.

First Lessons in Math © THE MONKEY SISTERS, INC.

Skill: Reviewing shapes

Name _____

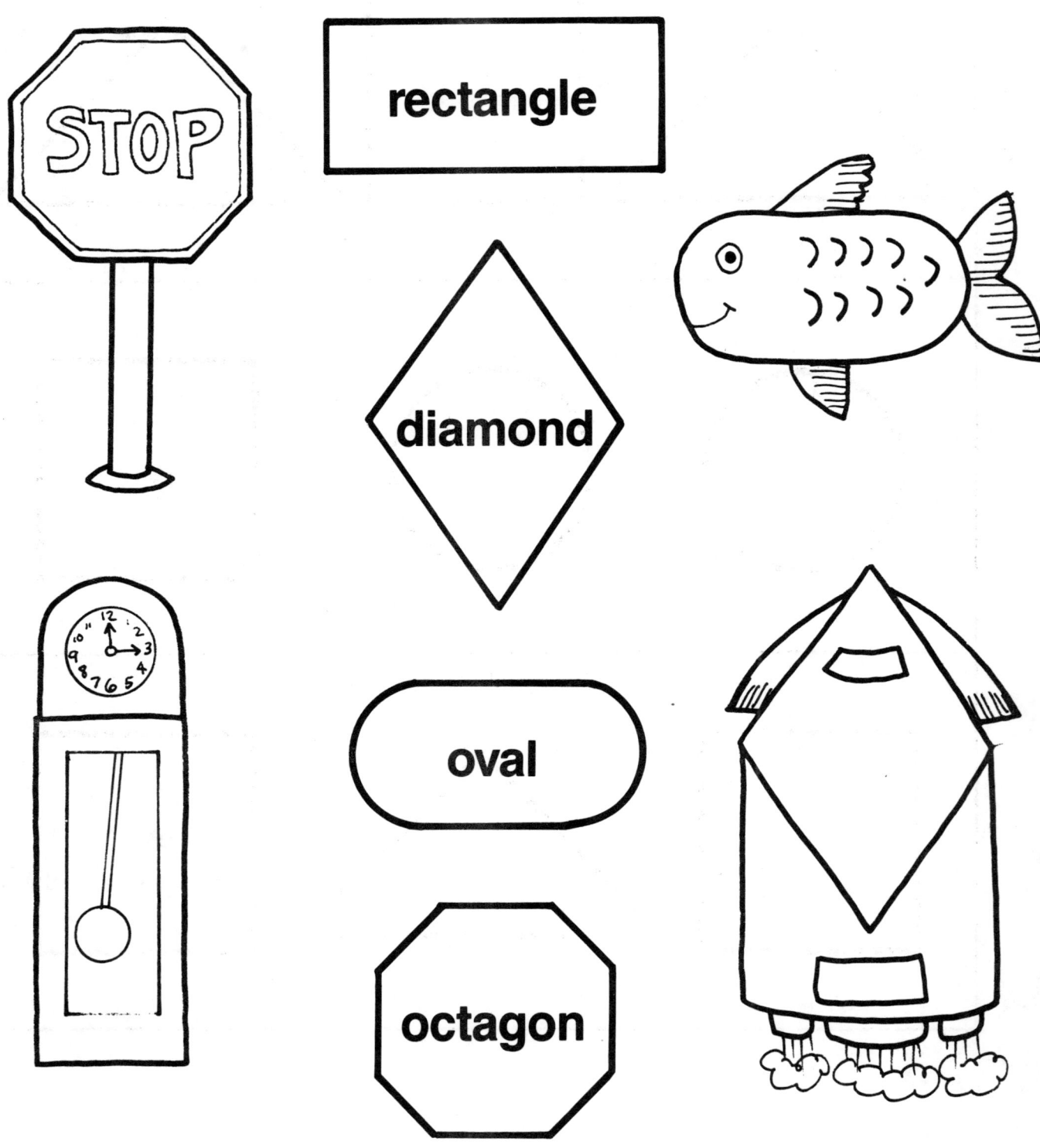

Directions: Children draw a line from the shape in the middle to the object that is made from that shape. Color both shapes the same color.

First Lessons in Math © THE MONKEY SISTERS, INC.

Skill: Reviewing shapes; following directions.

Name _____

Directions: Read orally to children: Color the large circle orange. Color the small circles brown. Color the triangle green. Color the square yellow. Color the rectangles blue. Color the octagon red. Color the ovals purple.

Skill: Telling time on the hour

Name _____

Digital Time

Directions: Children read numbers 1 to 12. Cut out number strip and clock. Cut slits at dotted lines. Insert strip between slits and move to read time on the hour.

First Lessons in Math © THE MONKEY SISTERS, INC.

Skill: Telling time on the hour

Name _____

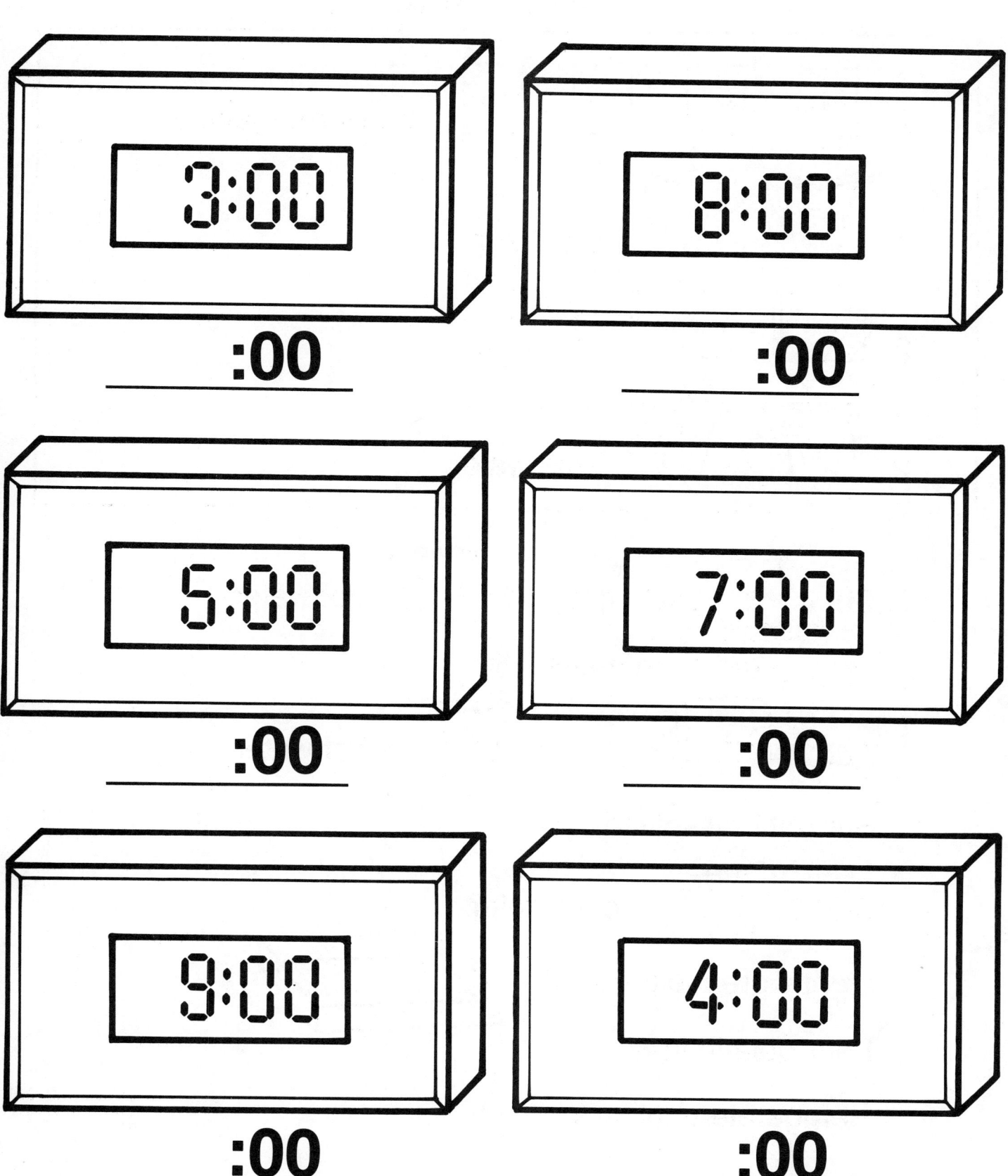

Directions: Children read the time on the clocks. Write the time on the line below the clock.

Skill: Measuring for recipes

Name _____

Finger Jello

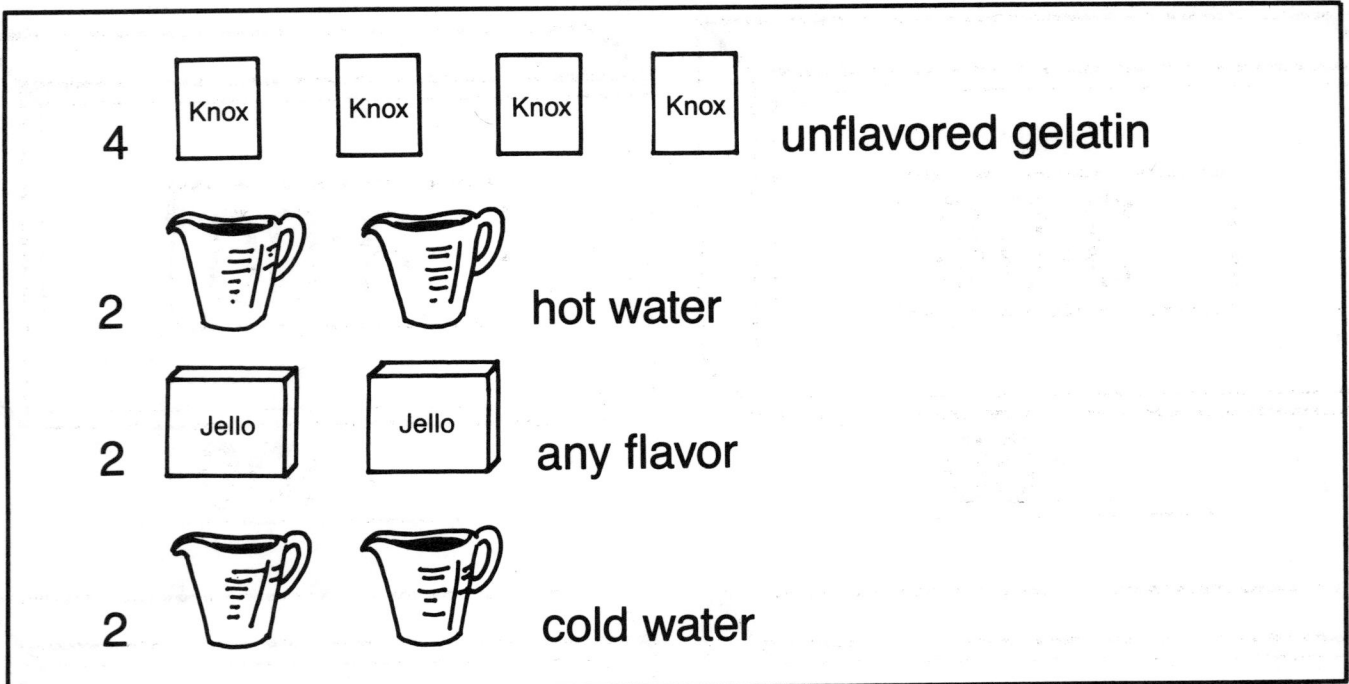

Stir 4 [Knox] packages in ½ [cup] hot water.

Let it stand 15 minutes.

Add 2 [Jello] and 1½ [cup]'s hot water.

Stir until dissolved.

Add 2 [cup]'s cold water.

Lightly grease a 9 x 13 [pan].

Pour gelatin in.

Refrigerate until firm.

Cut in squares to eat.

Directions: Prepare the recipe and have it for a snack in your class. Let children see that ingredients and measurements are according to directions.

Skill: Measuring ½ of objects

Name _____

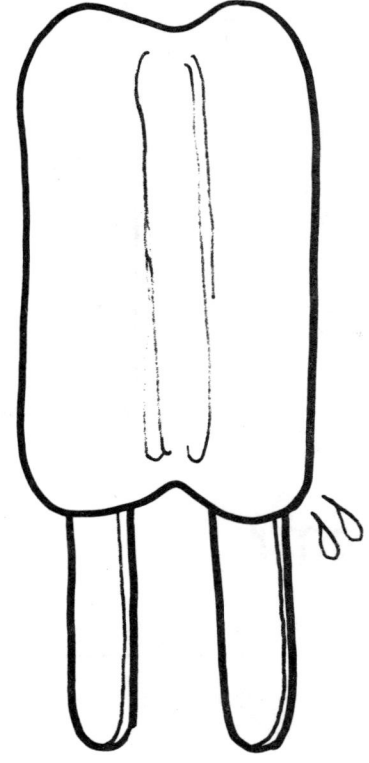

½

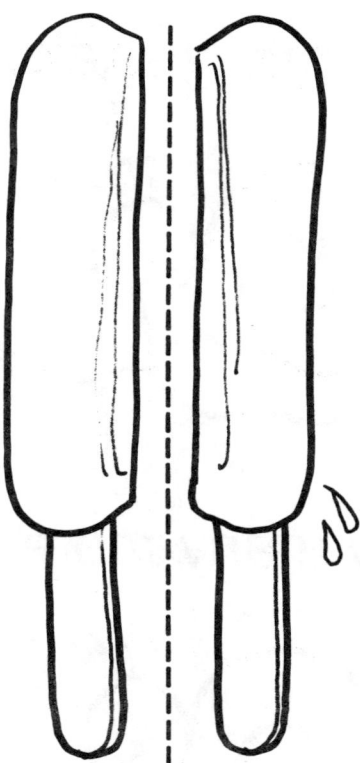

A whole popsicle **½ of a popsicle**

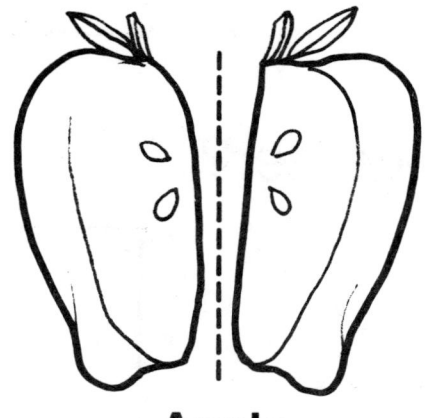

Apple

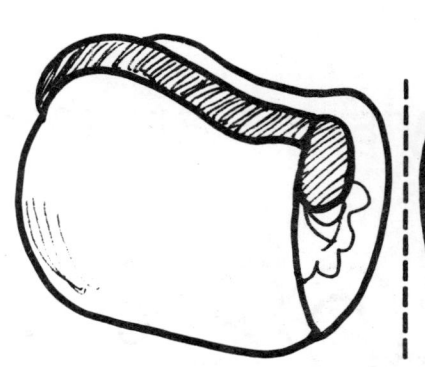

Hot dog

Soap

Cupcake

Directions: Children color ½ of each object.

First Lessons in Math © THE MONKEY SISTERS, INC.

Skill: Picture story problems—addition

How many snails are crawling?

How many more snails joined them?

How many snails are there altogether?

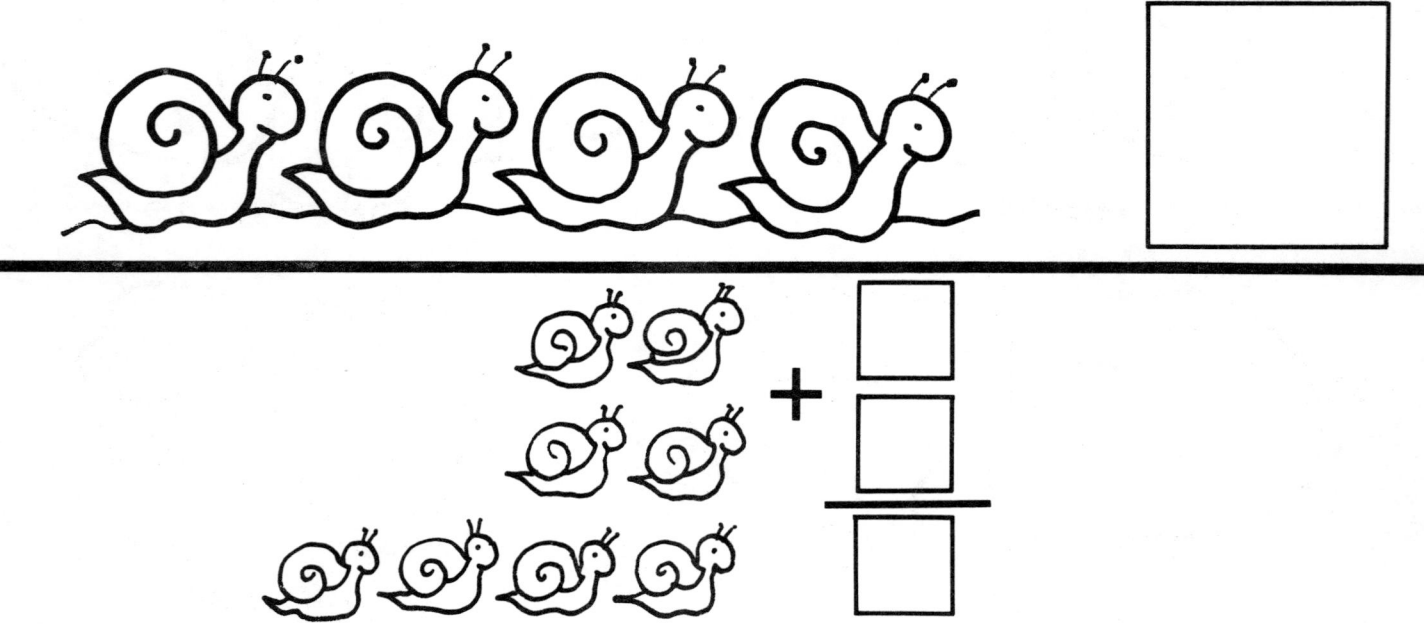

Directions: Read the questions to the children. Have squares filled in.
With the children, do the problem on the bottom of the page.

Skill: Picture story problems—subtraction

Name _____

How many ducks are swimming?

How many ducks stopped swimming?

How many ducks are still swimming?

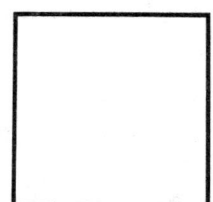

Directions: Read the questions to the children. Have squares filled in. Do the problem on the bottom with the children.

Skill: Graphing

Name _____

My Graph

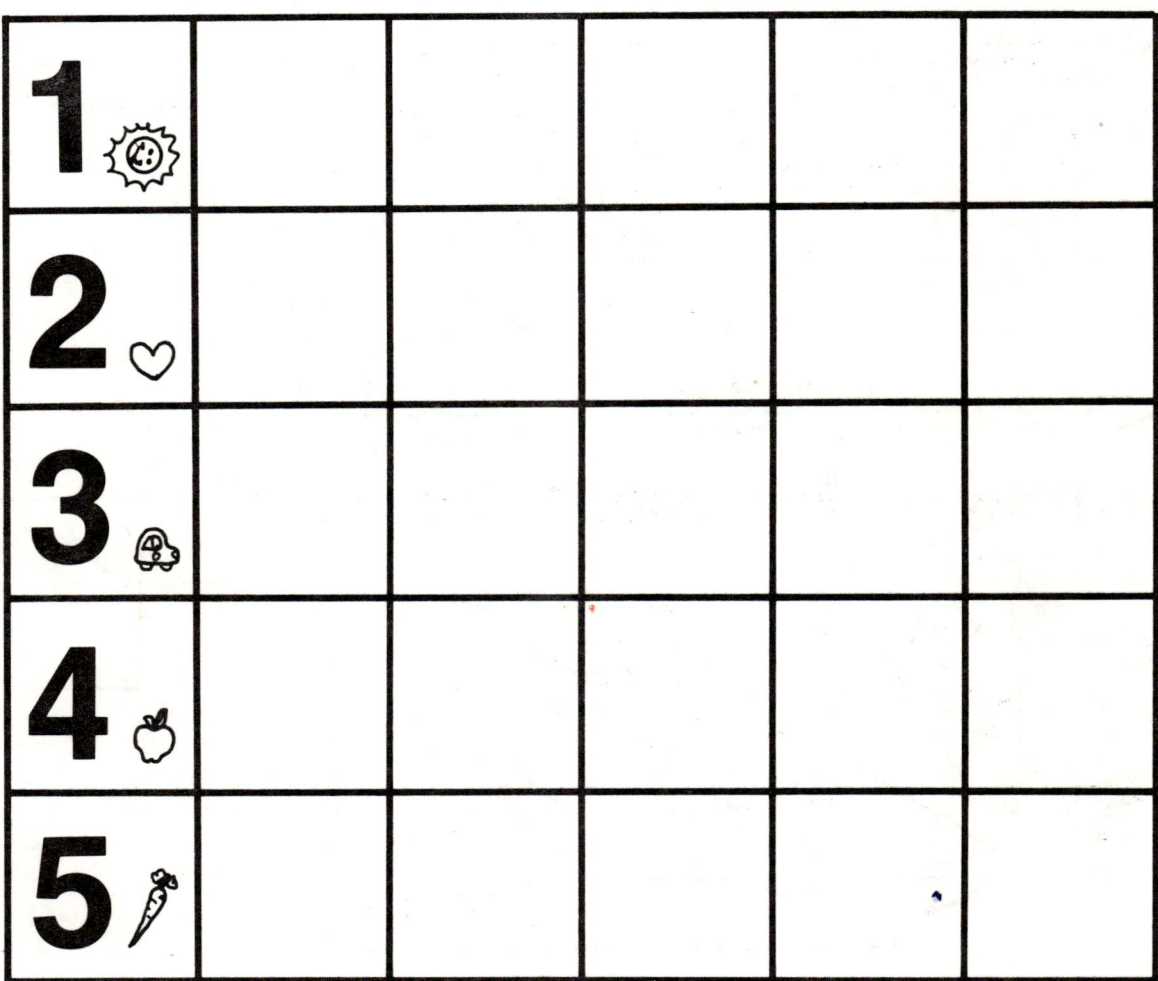

Directions: Children cut out squares with illustrations and paste on correct part of graph. When this is done, ask questions such as: How many cars are there? Are there more cars or hearts? How many apples are there? Are there more apples or carrots, etc.

First Lessons in Math © THE MONKEY SISTERS, INC.

Skill: Matching sets to numbers 1-10

Name _____

Number Chart

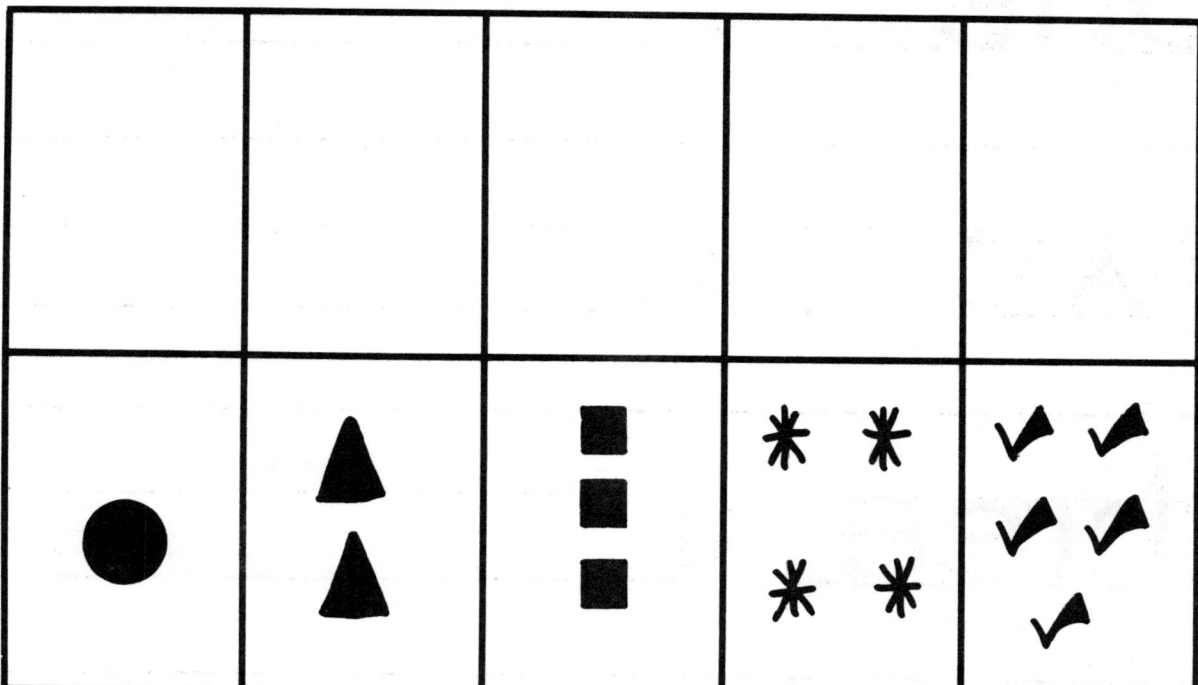

Directions: Children write in number to show how many are in each set.

First Lessons in Math © THE MONKEY SISTERS, INC.

Skill: Writing number words 1-5

Name _____

_____

one _____

two  _____

three  _____

four  _____

five  _____

Directions: Read the words with the children. Count the number of items on each line. Children write the word on the line to the right.

Skill: Writing number words 6-10 Name _____

six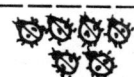

seven

eight

nine

ten

Directions: Read the words with the children. Count the number of items on each line. Children write the word on the line to the right.

First Lessons in Math © THE MONKEY SISTERS, INC.

See your local school supply dealer for these products by THE MONKEY SISTERS